This journal belongs to

_____

*D*ate

_____

> *You who have received so much love share it with others. Love others the way that God has loved you, with tenderness.*
>
> — MOTHER TERESA

> *You*, O Lord, are a compassionate and gracious God,
> slow to anger, abounding in love and faithfulness.
>
> PSALM 86:15 NIV

> *O*h, if we did but love others! How easily the least thing, the shutting of a door gently, the walking softly,…or the choice of a seat, so as to leave the most convenient to others, might become occasions of its exercise.
>
> — MÉRE ANGÉLIQUE ARNAULD

> Stay on good terms with each other, held together by love. Be ready with a meal or a bed when it's needed. Why, some have extended hospitality to angels without ever knowing it!
>
> HEBREWS 13:1-2 MSG

> *To worship rightly is to love each other,*
> *Each smile a hymn, each kindly deed a prayer.*
>
> — JOHN GREENLEAF WHITTIER

Be filled with the Spirit, speaking to one another in psalms and hymns and spiritual songs, singing and making melody in your heart to the Lord.

EPHESIANS 5:18-19 NKJV

> We are not responsible to feel, but we are responsible to love, and true spiritual love begins in the will.
>
> A. W. Tozer

For everything we know about God's Word is summed up in a single sentence: Love others as you love yourself. That's an act of true freedom.

GALATIANS 5:14 MSG

> *There is no surprise more magical than the surprise of being loved. It is God's finger on man's shoulder.*
>
> — CHARLES MORGAN

*May you have the power to understand,
as all God's people should, how wide,
how long, how high, and how deep His love is.*

EPHESIANS 3:18 NLT

> *T*oday, see if you can stretch your heart and expand your love so that it touches not only those to whom you can give it easily, but also those who need it so much.
>
> — DAPHNE ROSE KINGMA

> *Do not set your mind on high things, but associate with the humble. Do not be wise in your own opinion.... If it is possible, as much as depends on you, live peaceably with all men.*
>
> Romans 12:16, 18 NKJV

> *We should always remember that love is the highest gift of God. All of our revelations and gifts are little things compared to love.*
>
> — JOHN WESLEY

God so loved the world that He gave His only begotten Son, that whoever believes in Him should not perish but have everlasting life.

JOHN 3:16 NKJV

> *What is important is that one is capable of love.
> It is perhaps the only glimpse we are permitted of eternity.*
>
> — HELEN HAYES

For now we see in a mirror, dimly, but then face to face. Now I know in part, but then I shall know just as I also am known. And now abide faith, hope, love, these three; but the greatest of these is love.

1 Corinthians 13:12-13 nkjv

> *Love is a great thing, an altogether good gift, the only thing that makes burdens light and bears all that is hard with ease. It carries a weight without feeling it, and makes all that is bitter sweet and pleasant to the taste.*
>
> — THOMAS À KEMPIS

> This is my prayer for you: that your love will
> grow more and more; that you will have
> knowledge and understanding with your love.
>
> PHILIPPIANS 1:9 NCV

> *To love deeply in one direction makes us more loving in all others.*
>
> — ANNE-SOPHIE SWETCHINE

"*L*ove the Lord God with all your passion and prayer and intelligence and energy." And…"Love others as well as you love yourself." There is no other commandment that ranks with these.

Mark 12:29 the msg

> *Affection is not much good unless it is expressed....*
> *Putting an emotion into words gives it a life*
> *and a reality that otherwise it doesn't have.*
>
> — ARTHUR GORDON

*Don't just pretend to love others. Really love them.
Hate what is wrong. Hold tightly to what is good.*

Romans 12:9 NLT

> *When you love someone, you love the whole person, just as he or she is, and not as you would like them to be.*
>
> — LEO TOLSTOY

Simply love—love uncontaminated by self-interest and counterfeit faith, a life open to God.

1 Timothy 1:5 MSG

Love is a promise that is always kept, a fortune that can never be spent…. And this radiance that never fades, this mysterious and magical joy, is the greatest treasure of all— one known only by those who love.

Let us hold fast the confession of our hope without wavering, for He who promised is faithful.

HEBREWS 10:23 NKJV

> Though I have seen the oceans and mountains, though I have read great books and seen great works of art, though I have heard symphonies and tasted the best…foods, there is nothing greater or more beautiful than those people I love.
>
> CHRISTOPHER DE VINCK

I may have the gift of prophecy. I may understand all the secret things of God and have all knowledge, and I may have faith so great I can move mountains. But even with all these things, if I do not have love, then I am nothing.

1 Corinthians 13:2 ncv

> *Human love would never have the power it has were it not rooted in an express image of God.*
>
> — J. Mouroux

*D*ear friends, we should love each other, because love comes from God. Everyone who loves has become God's child and knows God. Whoever does not love does not know God, because God is love.

1 John 4:7-8 ncv

*L*ove, not liberty, is supreme. Love determines…conduct.
Love for God and concern for others are inseparable.

MARGARET BLOOM

> *Be humble, thinking of others as better than yourselves. Don't look out only for your own interests, but take an interest in others, too.*
>
> PHILIPPIANS 2:3-4 NLT

> *Treasure the love you receive above all. It will survive long after your gold and good health have vanished.*
>
> — OG MANDINO

> *S*tore your treasures in heaven, where moths and rust
> cannot destroy, and thieves do not break in and steal.
>
> MATTHEW 6:20 NLT

> *True love possesses the ability to see beyond....*
> *It goes beyond mere words. It sees beneath the veneer.*
> *Love focuses on the soul. Love sees another's soul*
> *in great need of help and sets compassion to work.*
>
> — CHARLES SWINDOLL

*Finally, all of you, live in harmony with one another;
be sympathetic, love as brothers, be compassionate and humble.*

1 Peter 3:8 niv

> **Y**ou have a unique message to deliver, a unique song to sing, a unique act of love to bestow. This message, this song, and this act of love have been entrusted exclusively to the one and only you.
>
> — JOHN POWELL

We all have different gifts, each of which came because of the grace God gave us.

ROMANS 12:6 NCV

> *Love* is extravagant in the price it is willing to pay,
> the time it is willing to give, the hardships it is willing to endure,
> and the strength it is willing to spend.
>
> JONI EARECKSON TADA

*C*hrist's love is greater than anyone can ever know, but I pray that you will be able to know that love. Then you can be filled with the fullness of God.

EPHESIANS 3:19 NCV

> God's heart is the most sensitive and tender of all.
> No act goes unnoticed, no matter how insignificant or small.
>
> — RICHARD J. FOSTER

*E*ye has not seen, nor ear heard, nor have entered into the heart of man the things which God has prepared for those who love Him.

1 Corinthians 2:9 nkjv

> *In true love it is not we who love…
> but it is God in us who loves them.*
>
> — SIMONE WEIL

This is what real love is: It is not our love for God; it is God's love for us.

1 JOHN 4:10 NCV

It's usually through our hard times…that we experience God in more intimate ways. We discover an unquenchable longing to know Him more. It's a passion that…pursues God and knows He is relentless in His pursuit of each one of us.

And so we know and rely on the love God has for us.
God is love. Whoever lives in love lives in God, and God in him.

1 JOHN 4:16 NIV

> God loves us for ourselves. He values our love more than He values galaxies of new created worlds.
>
> A. W. TOZER

Look at the birds. They don't plant or harvest, they don't have storerooms or barns, but God feeds them. And you are worth much more than birds.

LUKE 12:24 NCV

> *H*erein is grace and graciousness! Herein is love and loving kindness! How it opens to us the compassion of Jesus—so gentle, tender, considerate! We need never shrink back from His touch.
>
> — CHARLES H. SPURGEON

> I have loved you with an everlasting love;
> I have drawn you with loving-kindness.
>
> JEREMIAH 31:3 NIV

Let us love so well our work shall still be sweeter for our love, and still our love be sweeter for our work.

ELIZABETH BARRETT BROWNING

> *O*h! Teach us to live well! Teach us to live wisely
> and well!… Surprise us with love at daybreak;
> then we'll skip and dance all the day long.
>
> Psalm 90:12, 14 msg

*Love brings a new richness to life,
a higher intensity, a deeper meaning.*

May the Lord direct your hearts into God's love and Christ's perseverance.

2 THESSALONIANS 3:5 NIV

> *All people live, not by reason of any care they have for themselves, but by the love for them that is in other people.*
>
> LEO TOLSTOY

May the Lord make your love grow more and multiply for each other and for all people so that you will love others as we love you.

1 Thessalonians 3:12 NCV

> The love that we need is God Himself coming into our hearts. When the soul is perfected in love, it has such a sense of that love that it can rest in it for eternity.
>
> — ANDREW MURRAY

*May our Lord Jesus Christ Himself and God our Father,
who loved us and by His grace gave us eternal comfort
and a wonderful hope, comfort you and strengthen you
in every good thing you do and say.*

2 Thessalonians 2:16-17 NLT

If this one commandment were kept—"Love one another"—
I know that it would carry us a long way toward keeping
all the rest of our Lord's commands.

TERESA OF AVILA

*Treat one another justly. Love your neighbors.
Be compassionate with each other.*

ZECHARIAH 7:7 MSG

> *The supreme happiness of life is the conviction that we are loved, loved for ourselves, or rather, loved in spite of ourselves.*
>
> — Victor Hugo

It is clear to us, friends, that God not only loves you very much but also has put His hand on you for something special.

1 Thessalonians 1:4 msg

> *S*ome emotions don't make a lot of noise. It's hard to hear pride. Caring is real faint—like a heartbeat. And pure love— why, some days it's so quiet, you don't even know it's there.
>
> ERMA BOMBECK

The Lord your God is with you, He is mighty to save. He will take great delight in you, He will quiet you with His love, He will rejoice over you with singing.

ZEPHANIAH 3:17 NIV

> We who love our Lord, and we whose affections are set on the things that are heaven for us today—we voluntarily and gladly lay aside things that charm the world, so that we may be charmed and ravished with the things of heaven.
>
> — AMY CARMICHAEL

So we don't look at the troubles we can see now; rather, we fix our gaze on things that cannot be seen. For the things we see now will soon be gone, but the things we cannot see will last forever.

2 Corinthians 4:18 NLT

> *Love is the true means by which the world is enjoyed: our love to others, and others' love to us.*
>
> THOMAS TRAHERNE

I will tell of the Lord's unfailing love. I will praise the Lord for all He has done. I will rejoice in His great goodness.

Isaiah 63:7 NLT

> *I think that love is the only spiritual power that can overcome the self-centeredness that is inherent in being alive.*
>
> — ARNOLD TOYNBEE

My dear children, let's not just talk about love; let's practice real love. This is the only way we'll know we're living truly, living in God's reality.

1 John 3:18 msg

Love builds memories that endure, to be treasured up as hints of what shall be hereafter.

BEDE JARRET

*G*et for yourselves purses that will not wear out, the treasure in heaven that never runs out, where thieves can't steal and moths can't destroy. Your heart will be where your treasure is.

Luke 12:33-34 ncv

His tenderness in the springing grass,
His beauty in the flowers,
His living love in the sun above—
All here, and near, and ours.

CHARLOTTE PERKINS GILMAN

*B*ecause I am God, your personal God,…your Savior.
I paid a huge price for you…. That's how much you mean to Me!
That's how much I love you! I'd sell off the whole world
to get you back, trade the creation just for you.

Isaiah 43:3-4 msg

*O*nly He who created the wonders of the world
entwines hearts in an eternal way.

Then Christ will make His home in your hearts as you trust in Him. Your roots will grow down into God's love and keep you strong.

EPHESIANS 3:17 NLT

> We never live so intensely as when we love strongly.
> We never realize ourselves so vividly as when
> we are in the full glow of love for others.
>
> — WALTER RAUSCHENBUSCH

Patience produces character, and character produces hope. And this hope will never disappoint us, because God has poured out His love to fill our hearts.

ROMANS 5:4-5 NCV

> *After the friendship of God, a friend's affection is the greatest treasure here below.*

For in Christ Jesus…the only thing that counts is faith expressing itself through love.

GALATIANS 5:6 NIV

> *L*ove has been called the most effective motivational force in all the world. When love is at work in us, it is remarkable how giving and forgiving, understanding and tolerant we can be.
>
> — CHARLES SWINDOLL

> Live a life of love just as Christ loved us and gave Himself for us as a sweet-smelling offering and sacrifice to God.
>
> Ephesians 5:2 ncv

God loves you…whether you like it or not.

For I am persuaded that neither death nor life, nor angels nor principalities nor powers, nor things present nor things to come, nor height nor depth, nor any other created thing, shall be able to separate us from the love of God.

ROMANS 8:38-39 NKJV

> *Love is the only passion which includes in its dreams the happiness of someone else.*
>
> — ALPHONSE KARR

*But let everyone who trusts You be happy;
let them sing glad songs forever. Protect those who
love You and who are happy because of You.*

PSALM 5:11 NCV

To love anyone is nothing else than to wish that person good.

THOMAS AQUINAS

If your gift is to encourage others, be encouraging. If it is giving, give generously.… And if you have a gift for showing kindness to others, do it gladly.

Romans 12:8 nlt

> When one has once fully entered the realm of love,
> the world—no matter how imperfect—becomes rich
> and beautiful, for it consists solely of opportunities for love.
>
> — Søren Kierkegaard

> *This is how everyone will recognize that you are My disciples—
> when they see the love you have for each other.*
>
> JOHN 13:35 MSG

> *The highest love of all finds its fulfillment not in what it keeps, but in what it gives.*
>
> — FATHER ANDREW SDC

*Go after a life of love as if your life depended on it—
because it does. Give yourselves to the gifts
God gives you. Most of all, try to proclaim His truth.*

1 Corinthians 14:1 msg

> *There isn't a man or a woman anywhere, I am convinced, who does not long for tenderness.*
>
> — ELISABETH ELLIOT

*R*emember, O Lord, Your tender mercies and Your lovingkindnesses, for they are from of old.

Psalm 25:6 nkjv

> *Though we do not have our Lord with us in bodily presence, we have our neighbor, who, for the ends of love and loving service, is as good as our Lord Himself.*
>
> — Teresa of Avila

Then the King will answer, "I tell you the truth, anything you did for even the least of My people here, you also did for Me."

Matthew 25:40 ncv

> *Real* love loves for love's sake
> and not because the loved one is lovable.
>
> — EUGENIA PRICE

But above all these things put on love, which is the bond of perfection.

COLOSSIANS 3:14 NKJV

*L*ove never thinks in terms of "how little," but always in terms of "how much." Love gives, love knows, and love lasts.

JONI EARECKSON TADA

*May what our Master Jesus Christ gives freely
be deeply and personally yours, my friends.*

GALATIANS 6:18 MSG

*Heaven comes down to touch us
when we find ourselves safe in the heart of another.*

If you have any encouragement from being united with Christ,
if any comfort from His love,…if any tenderness and compassion,
then make my joy complete by being like-minded,
having the same love, being one in spirit and purpose.

PHILIPPIANS 2:1-2 NIV

> *L*ove seeks one thing only: the good of the one loved.
> It leaves all the other secondary effects to take care
> of themselves. Love, therefore, is its own reward.
>
> THOMAS MERTON

May the Lord be loyal to you in return and reward you with His unfailing love!

2 Samuel 2:6 nlt

> *T*o love by freely giving is its own reward.
> To be possessed by love and to in turn give love away
> is to find the secret of abundant life.
>
> — GLORIA GAITHER

I have come that they may have life, and that they may have it more abundantly.

JOHN 10:10 NKJV

> *L*ove is that condition in which the happiness
> of another person is essential to your own.
>
> ROBERT A. HEINLEIN

Because we loved you, we were happy to share not only God's Good News with you, but even our own lives. You had become so dear to us!

1 Thessalonians 2:8 NCV

> *How far you go in life depends on your being tender with the young, compassionate with the aged, sympathetic with the striving, and tolerant of the weak and the strong—because someday in life you will be all of these.*
>
> — GEORGE WASHINGTON CARVER

You must be compassionate, just as your Father is compassionate.

LUKE 6:36 NLT

> *You can give without loving, but you cannot love without giving.*
> — AMY CARMICHAEL

If I gave everything I have to the poor and even sacrificed my body, I could boast about it; but if I didn't love others, I would have gained nothing.

1 Corinthians 13:3 NLT

> We never love our neighbor so truly as when our love for him is prompted by the love of God.
>
> — FRANÇOIS FÉNELON

Now may the God of patience and comfort grant you to be like-minded toward one another, according to Christ Jesus.

ROMANS 15:5 NKJV

> *ℒove is the seed of all hope. It is the enticement to trust, to risk, to try, to go on.*
>
> GLORIA GAITHER

*God has made everything beautiful for its own time.
He has planted eternity in the human heart.*

ECCLESIASTES 3:11 NLT

*Love makes burdens lighter, because you divide them.
It makes joys more intense, because you share them.
It makes you stronger, so that you can reach out and become involved
with life in ways you dared not risk alone.*

It is absolutely clear that God has called you to a free life.... Use your freedom to serve one another in love; that's how freedom grows.

GALATIANS 5:13 MSG

> **M**ake your service of love a beautiful thing;
> want nothing else, fear nothing else and let love be
> free to become what love truly is.
>
> HADEWIJCH OF ANTWERP

Be kindly affectionate to one another with brotherly love,
in honor giving preference to one another.

Romans 12:10 NKJV

> *L*ove is the only force capable
> of transforming an enemy into a friend.
>
> — MARTIN LUTHER KING JR.

*You're familiar with the old written law, Love your friend....
I'm telling you to love your enemies. Let them bring out
the best in you, not the worst.... For then you are working
out of your true selves, your God-created selves.*

MATTHEW 5:43-45 MSG

> *It is only by thinking about great and good things that we come to love them, and it is only by loving them [and] longing for them that we…seek after them; and it is only by seeking after them that they become ours.*
>
> HENRY VAN DYKE

Seek the Lord your God, and you will find Him if you seek Him with all your heart and with all your soul.

DEUTERONOMY 4:29 NKJV

> *Duty makes us do things well,
> but love makes us do them beautifully.*
>
> — PHILLIPS BROOKS

They share freely and give generously to those in need.
Their good deeds will be remembered forever.
They will have influence and honor.

Psalm 112:9 NLT

> *It is not enough to love those who are near and dear to us.
> We must show them that we do so.*
>
> — LORD AVEBURY

We continually remember before our God and Father your work produced by faith, your labor prompted by love, and your endurance inspired by hope in our Lord Jesus Christ.

1 THESSALONIANS 1:3 NIV

> The one who truly loves in spirit…cares nothing whether he receives the affection of another or not…for the sake of God's love, will love others a great deal. They will love with greater compassion and greater intensity.
>
> — Teresa of Avila

With Your unfailing love You lead the people You have redeemed.
In Your might, You guide them to Your sacred home.

Exodus 15:13 NLT

> *There is a time for risky love. There is a time for extravagant gestures. There is a time to pour out your affections on one you love. And when the time comes—seize it, don't miss it.*
>
> MAX LUCADO

If you spend yourselves in behalf of the hungry and satisfy the needs of the oppressed, then your light will rise in the darkness, and your night will become like the noonday.

ISAIAH 58:10 NIV

> *Trying to find yourself within yourself is like peeling the layers off an onion. When you finish you have nothing but a pile of peelings. The only way to find yourself is to go outside of yourself and love another.*
>
> — RHONDA S. HOGAN

*I*nvestigate my life, O God, find out everything about me;
cross-examine and test me, get a clear picture of what
I'm about;…then guide me on the road to eternal life.

Psalm 139:23–24 msg

> *Affection is the most satisfying reward one can receive. It costs nothing, is readily available, and provides great encouragement.*

Your love has given me great joy and encouragement, because you…have refreshed the hearts of the saints.

Philemon 1:7 niv

> When the heart is pure it cannot help loving,
> because it has discovered the source of love which is God.
>
> — JEAN-MARIE BAPTISTE VIANNEY

*For from Him and through Him and to Him are all things.
To Him be the glory forever! Amen.*

ROMANS 11:36 NIV

*Love is a fabric which never fades,
no matter how often it is washed in the waters of adversity.*

*T*hank the Lord because He is good. His love continues forever.... They were hungry and thirsty, and they were discouraged. In their misery they cried out to the Lord, and He saved them from their troubles.

Psalm 107:1, 5-6 ncv

> *One who loves is borne on wings; he runs, and is filled with joy; he is free and unrestricted. He gives all to receive all, and he has all in all; for beyond all things he rests in the one highest thing, from Whom streams all that is good.*
>
> — THOMAS À KEMPIS

Those who wait on the Lord shall renew their strength; they shall mount up with wings like eagles, they shall run and not be weary, they shall walk and not faint.

Isaiah 40:31 NKJV

Simply Ellie
Brentwood, TN 37027
EllieClaire.com
Ellie Claire is a registered trademark of Worthy Media, Inc.

Copyright © 2014 by Ellie Claire® Gift & Paper Expressions
Published by Ellie Claire, an imprint of Worthy Publishing Group, a division of Worthy Media, Inc.

All rights reserved. No part of this book may be reproduced in any form, except for brief quotations in printed reviews, without permission in writing from the publisher.

Scripture quotations are taken from the following sources: The Holy Bible, New International Version®, NIV®. Copyright © 1973, 1978, 1984, 2011 by Biblica, Inc.™ Used by permission of Zondervan. All rights reserved worldwide. The Holy Bible, New King James Version (NKJV). Copyright © 1982 by Thomas Nelson, Inc. Used by permission. The Holy Bible, New Living Translation (NLT), copyright 1996, 2004, 2007 by Tyndale House Foundation. Used by permission of Tyndale House Publishers, Inc., Carol Stream, Illinois 60188. *The Message* (MSG). Copyright © 1993, 1994, 1995, 1996, 2000, 2001, 2002 by Eugene Peterson. Used by permission of NavPress, Colorado Springs, CO. The New Century Version® (NCV). Copyright © 1987, 1988, 1991 by Thomas Nelson, Inc. Used by permission. All rights reserved.

Stock or custom editions of Ellie Claire titles may be purchased in bulk for educational, business, ministry, fundraising, or sales promotional use. For information, please e-mail info@EllieClaire.com

Compiled by Barbara Farmer
Printed in China

1 2 3 4 5 6 7 8 9 – 19 18 17 16 15 14